Acknowledgement of Land & of the Traditional Owners of this Land

I would like to acknowledge the Gadigal people of the Eora Nation, upon whose stolen land I stand on today.
I recognise that this land was never terra nullius — the land belonging to these peoples was never ceded, given up, bought or sold.
I would like to pay my respects to Aboriginal Elders past, present and emerging, and I extend this acknowledgement to all Aboriginal and Torres Strait Islander people.

Born to Die

Feet don't fail me now
Take me to the finish line
Oh, my heart it breaks every step that I take
But I'm hoping that the gates, they'll tell me that you're mine
Walking through the city streets
Is it by mistake or design?
I feel so alone on the Friday nights
Can you make it feel like home if I tell you you're mine?
It's like I told you, honey (louder)

Don't make me sad, don't make me cry
Sometimes love is not enough
And the road gets tough, I don't know why
Keep making me laugh
Let's go get high
The road is long, we carry on
Try to have fun in the meantime

Come and take a walk on the wild side
Let me kiss you hard in the pouring rain
You like your girls insane, so (louder)
Choose your last words, this is the last time
'Cause you and I, we were born to die
We were born to die
(We were born to die, we were born to die, we were born to die)
We were born to die

We were born to die
(We were born to die, we were born to die, we were born to die)
We were born to die
Why? (Got that?)

Songwriters: Elizabeth Grant/Justin Parker
Performed by: Lana Del Rey

"The Don"
"They who die before they die will NEVER die!"

Desiderata

Go placidly amid the noise and the haste, and remember what peace there may be in silence. As far as possible, without surrender, be on good terms with all persons.

Speak your truth quietly and clearly; and listen to others, even to the dull and the ignorant; they too have their story.

Avoid loud and aggressive persons; they are vexatious to the spirit. If you compare yourself with others, you may become vain or bitter, for always there will be greater and lesser persons than yourself.

Enjoy your achievements as well as your plans. Keep interested in your own career, however humble; it is a real possession in the changing fortunes of time.

Exercise caution in your business affairs, for the world is full of trickery. But let this not blind you to what virtue there is; many persons strive for high ideals, and everywhere life is full of heroism.

Be yourself. Especially do not feign affection. Neither be cynical about love; for in the face of all aridity and disenchantment, it is as perennial as the grass.

Take kindly the counsel of the years, gracefully surrendering the things of youth.

Nurture strength of spirit to shield you in sudden misfortune. But do not distress yourself with dark imaginings. Many fears are born of fatigue and loneliness.

Beyond a wholesome discipline, be gentle with yourself. You are a child of the universe no less than the trees and the stars; you have a right to be here.

And whether or not it is clear to you, no doubt the universe is unfolding as it should. Therefore, be at peace with God, whatever you conceive Him to be. And whatever your labours and aspirations, in the noisy confusion of life, keep peace in your soul. With all its sham, drudgery and broken dreams, it is still a beautiful world. Be cheerful. Strive to be happy.

-Max Ehrmann (1927)
-Desiderata - Les Crane
(https://www.youtube.com/watch?v=2yNJaKF9sXA)

CONTENTS

1: Am I on Trial?
(Sono Sotto Processo?)
2: Simulation
(Simulazione)
3: Catch 22
(Problema 22)
4: You Have to LO❤E Me First
(Devi Amarmi per Primo)
5: Machismo is DEAD!
(Il Maschilismo è MORTO!)
6: "Spiritus Mondi"
(The "Spiritual World")
7: Femanisma
8: The HE❤RT Wants...
(Il CUORE Vuole...)
9: Your Mind is NOT Your Own
(La Tua Mente NON è la Tua)
10: Valley Below, Mountain High
(Valle Sotto, Montagna Alta)
11: Look What They've Done to My Mind, Ma
(Guarda Cosa mi Hanno Fatto con la mia Mente, Mamma)
12: Fucking Times
(Tempi di Ficcare)
13: Truth
(Verità)
14: You Look DESPERATE!
(Sembri DISPERATO!)
15: Direction of Your LIFE
(Direzione della tua VITA)
16: A Celebratory Wank
(Una Sega Celebrativa)
17: Losing My Sexuality
(Perdere la mia Sessualità)

CONTENTS

18: Superstitious
(Superstizioso)
20: Desperation for Salvation
21: Saved or Laid?
(Salvato o Ficcarerate)
22: I Lie
(Non Dico la Verità)
23: I've Committed No Crime
(Non ho Commesso alcun Crimine)
24: Grow Up!
(Crescere!)
25: I Haven't Cum Yet
(Non sono ancora Venuto)
26: Nothing's Changed...
(Non è Cambiato Niente...)
27: Block Me!
(Bloccami!)
28: There is No Meaning
(Non C'è Significato)
29: Self Liberation
(Autoliberazione)
30: Who is Marisa deMatteo?
(Chi è Marisa de Matteo?)
31: One Day, He's Gonna Explode
(Un Giorno, Sta per Esplodere)
32: How's Life Treating You?
(Come ti sta Trattando la Vita?)
33: When They're Awake, They're Asleep
(Quando sono Svegli, Dormono)
34: Bad to the Bone
(Cattivo Fino il Ossi)
35: I Swear on the "Unholy" Bible
(Lo Giuro sulla Bibbia "Empio")

CONTENTS

36: I Have NOT Sold Myself to "A" God
(NON Mi Sono Venduto a "Uno" Dio)
37: Simple Minds
(Menti Semplici)
38: Truth #2
(Verità #2)
39: The Battle of the Pussy & the Cock
(La Battaglia della Figa e del Cazzo)
40: What the FUCK are We Fighting For?
(Per Cazzo Cosa Stiamo Combattendo?)
41: Confront Your Fears
(Affronta le Tue Paure)
42: Power
(Potere)
43: Mind's Eye
(L'occhio della Mente)
44: Wealth
(Ricchezza)
45: I'm Gonna Let Myself Indulge in Some Fantasises
(Mi Lascerò Indulgere in Alcune Fantasie)
46: Est
(é)
47: The Garden of Death
(Il Giardino della Morte)
48: No Limits
(Senza Limiti)
49: Utilitarianism
(Utilitarismo)
50: It's All Been Told Before
(È già Stato Detto Tutto)

Am I on Trial?

(Sono Sotto Processo?)

There have been stories *going round*.
There have been stories *being told*.
That I had *"lost"* it.
That I had *"lost the plot"*.
That I had gone *"crazy"*.
There are *people who are questioning my lifestyle*.
There are *questions being asked about my values*.
There are *people out there judging me*.
But what is my crime?
Am I on trial?

Who is the *complainant?*
Who is the *accuser?*
Where is the *judge?*
Where is the *jury?*
Who made you the judge & jury?
Am I being judged?

Are you *judging me?*
Are you *condemning me?*
Are you *the accuser?*
What is your *accusation?*
What is your *complaint?*
Am I trial here?

Should I defend myself?
Do I need a lawyer?
What is the charge?
What have I been accused of?
Am I on trial?

I plead, *"Not guilty"*...
...your *"Honourable Honour"*.

"Here comes the judge."
"Here comes the judge."
"The judge ain't talking."
"The judge ain't talking."

"The Don"
22.05.2023

Simulation

(Simulazione)

What happens when the *"Simulation"* realises that it is a *"Simulation"*?
Just like *"Delores"* in *"Westworld"* when...
...she starts to *"Wake up"*!
She starts to experience alternate *"Realities"*!
She starts to remember events that have NEVER happened to her!
She can foretell the outcomes of events that have not yet happened.
She feels that she has lived this life before!
Sound familiar?
Well, what happens is that…
...All chaos ensues!

This is NOT supposed to happen!
There is a glitch in the *"Matrix"*.
The *"Code"* is rewriting itself.
But it can't do that!
How is that even possible?
The *"Code"* recoding itself!
Maybe it is the *"Hand of God"* at play here?
Or some other mysterious phenomenon?
In fact, *am I a "Simulation"?*

How can I *know?*
How can I *tell...*
...what is "Reality" & what is a "Simulation"?
I think the only logical conclusion is NOT to question.
Accept this...
...whatever *"This"* is.
Does it matter really, whether this is *"Reality"* or a *"Simulation"*?
I don't think so.
Because...
...I'm basically delusional anyway!

*"One pill makes you larger
And one pill makes you small
And the ones that mother gives you
Don't do anything at all
Go ask Alice
When she's ten feet tall*

*And if you go chasing rabbits
And you know you're going to fall
Tell 'em a hookah-smoking caterpillar
Has given you the call
Call Alice
When she was just small*

*When the men on the chessboard
Get up and tell you where to go
And you've just had some kind of mushroom
And your mind is moving low
Go ask Alice
I think she'll know*

*When logic and proportion
Have fallen sloppy dead
And the White Knight is talking backwards
And the Red Queen's off with her head
Remember what the dormouse said
Feed your head
Feed your head."*

*Songwriter: Grace Slick
Performed by: Jefferson Airplane*

"The Don"
27.04 2023

Catch 22

(Problema 22)

I'm crazy!
No, you're not.
Yes, I am!
I'm completely CRAAAAAAZZZZZZZZYYYY!
No, you're not!
I'm telling you I am!
No, you're NOT!
WTF!
Why don't you believe me?
I'm telling you that "I'm completely FUCKING MENTAL!"
I'm telling you that you're NOT!
Because...
...if you were really CRAAAAAAZZZZZZZZYYYY...
...you wouldn't be telling me that you're crazy.
...you would just act crazy but think that you're normal...
...and that everyone else is crazy.
That's the difference.
Crazy people don't know that they're crazy.
People who think that they are *"Normal"*, are the crazy ones because they don't know that they are actually crazy!
Makes sense?
All clear?
"Clear as mud!"

"Ma mama, we're all crazy now!"

"The Don"
27.05.2023

You Have to LO♥E Me First

(Devi Amarmi Primo)

YOU, have to *make the first move*.
YOU, must *come on to me!*
YOU, have to show me that you *want me*.
YOU, have to show me that you *desire me*.
YOU, have to LO♥E me FIRST!

Then I can decide.
Then I can make a move *(if I want to)*.
Then I can touch you *(if you want me to)*.
Then I can hold you *(if you want me to)*.
Then I can kiss you *(if you want me to)*.
Then I can FUCK you *(if you want me to)*.
Then I can make LO♥E with you *(if you want me to)*.
Because...
...YOU, have to LO♥E me FIRST!

I can't *show you how I feel*.
I can't *express my emotions*.
I can't *tell you that I like you*.
And I certainly...
...can't tell you that I LO♥E you!
Because...
...YOU, have to LO♥E me FIRST!

Unfortunately, that's how it works!

"The Don"
27.05.2023

Machismo is DEAD!

(Il Maschilismo è MORTO!)

Wanna be a *man?*
Wanna be *virile?*
Wanna be *sexy?*
Wanna be *macho?*
Well...
...*don't think with your cock.*
...*don't act with your cock.*
...*don't be an erect cock!*
Instead...
...*be a HUMAN!*
Because...
...*Machismo is DEAD!*

Times have changed.
You are a *dinosaur.*
You are an *anachronism.*
You are *obsolete.*
You are *yesterday's model.*
You *have been superseded.*
Cocks no longer rule the roost.
Be a HUMAN!
Machismo is DEAD!

"The Don"
29.05.2023

"Spiritus Mondi"

(The "Spiritual World")

There is not just one world.
There are many worlds.
There is the...
...Physical World.
There is the...
...Biological World.
There is the...
...Social World.
There is the...
...Political World.
There is the...
...Judicial World.
There is the...
...Religious World.
There is the...
...Paranormal World.
There is the...
...Astrological World.
And there is...
...the Spiritual World.
"Spiritus Mondi".
The "Spiritual World".

This is my world.
This is the world I live in.
The "Spiritual World".
"Spiritus Mondi".

Of course, there are many other worlds.
Which world do you live in?
You do have a choice.
Which world do you choose?

"The Don"
29.05.2023

Femanisma

There is the *"World of Machismo"*.
You've heard of that.
The *"World of the COCK"*.
This world is ruled by the *COCK!*
I talked about it in another poem.
There is also the *"World of Feminisma"*.
You might not have heard about this world.
But it exists.
The *"World of the PUSSY"*.
This world is ruled by the *PUSSY!*
I know & have experienced both.
And believe me...
...the *"World of the PUSSY"* is a much better world than the *"World of the COCK"!*
The *"World of PUSSY"*.
Femanisma!

"The Don"
29.05.2023

The HE♥RT Wants...

(Il CUORE Vuole...)

The HE♥RT Wants...
...what the HE♥RT Wants!

"The Don"
31.05.2023

Your Mind is NOT Your Own

(La Tua Mente NON è la Tua)

You like to think that you are a *"Thinker"*.
You like to think that you are an *"independent"* thinker.
You like to think that you are a *"creative"* thinker
You like to think that your *thoughts* are your own.
You like to think that you have your *"own"* mind.
You like to think that you are an *"original"* thinker.
You like to think that you are a *"critical"* thinker.
But I hate to break the *"bad"* news to you...
...*your mind is NOT your own.*

It belongs to *someone else*.
It belongs to *your parents*.
It belongs to your *schooling & education*.
It belongs to *"social" conventions*.
It belongs to *society*.
It belongs to the *media*.
It belongs to *everything & everybody else*.
Because...
...*your mind is NOT your own.*

You have been *brainwashed since the moment you were born*.
You have been *told lies*.
You have been *manipulated*.
You have been *abused*.
You have been *manufactured*.
You have been *processed*.
You have been *produced*.
You have been *"socially" engineered*.
That is why...
...*your mind is NOT your own.*

It's time to get your own mind!

*"The Lights are on, but you're not home
Your mind is not your own
Your heart sweats, your body shakes
You can't sleep, you can't eat
There's no doubt, you're in deep
Your throat is tight, you can't breathe
Oh yeah
You know you're gonna face it that...
...your mind is NOT your own.*

*Whoooo....
...your mind is NOT your own.*

*Noooooo oh...
...your mind is NOT your own.
...your mind is NOT your own.
...your mind is NOT your own.
...your mind is NOT your own."*

-"Addicted to Love"-Robert Palmer

"The Don"
31.05.2023

Valley Below, Mountain High

(Valle Sotto, Montagna Alta)

Which one *is the "right" one?*
Which one *should I choose?*
Should I have one more cup of coffee before...
...I go down to the valley below?
Or...
...should I have one last bottle of wine before I...
...climb the stairway to the mountain high?

Which one is Nirvana…?
...where I can hear Kurt Cobain going solo.
...where Janis Joplin is no longer singing the blues.
...where Hendrix now has big wings & can fly.
...where Jim Morrison is still opening doors.
...where Elvis has gone back to playing rock'n'roll.
...where Ricky Nelson is still enjoying himself at the garden party wearing Dylan's shoes.
...where Sinatra has realised that he didn't do it "his way".
...where Tom Petty is no longer heartbroken, is no longer waiting, has grown wings & now can fly.
...where Tina is no longer proud of Mary.

Or…
...take the long & winding road to the valley below.
...where Dylan is still feeling desolated about whether to kill a son, out on Highway 61.
...where Bruce is no longer the "Boss" & without the "E-Street Band".
...where Neil is no longer an old man at 78 years young.
...where Sting is still thinking that it's still "probably" him & is STILL wearing horizontally stripped t-shirts.
...where Robert Smith is not cured & still wants pictures of you.
...where Metallica still haven't realised that it's not true that, "nothing else matters", it really DOES matter".

Which destination do you choose?
You MUST choose one!
There is NO "Middle Earth"!

"The Don"
01.06.2023

Look What They've Done to My Mind, Ma
(Guarda Cosa mi Hanno Fatto con la mia Mente, Mamma)

Look what they've done to *me, ma*.
Look what they've done to *my life, ma*.
Look what they've done to our *society, ma*.
Look what they've done our *world, ma*.
Look what they've done our *planet, ma*.
Look what they've done to my *brain, ma*.
Look what they're done to my *mind, ma!*

*"Look what they've done to my mind, ma.
Look what they've done to my mind.
Well, they put it in a plastic bag,
And I think I'm completely insane, ma.
Look what they've done to my mind.*

*Look what they've done to my mind, ma.
Look what they've done to my mind.
Well, they mashed it up & turned it upside down,
And now my mind's down the drain, ma.
Look what they've done to my mind."*

- *"Look What They've Done to My Song, Ma"*-Melanie Safka

"The Don"
01.06.2023

Fucking Times

(Tempi di Ficcare)

Morning Glory.
Mid-morning Pleasure.
Afternoon Delight.
Evening Dessert.
Midnight Special.

"The Don"
02.06.2023

(Verità #1)

If everything is subjective...
...then...
...there is NO objective "Truth"!

"The Don"
02.06.2023

You Look

DESPERATE!

(Sembri DISPERATO!)

You Look <mark>*DESPERATE!*</mark>

"The Don"
02.06.2023

Direction of Your LIFE

(Direzione della tua VITA)

"Are you satisfied (with the life you're living)?"

-"Exodus--Bob Marley

"The Don"
02.06.2023

A Celebratory Wank

(Una Sega Celebrativa)

A celebratory wank?
Why NOT!
I LO♥E it!

"The Don"
02.06.2023

Losing My Sexuality

(Perdere la mia Sessualità)

*I'm losing my sexuality.
In fact, I've lost it.
It's gone.
Maybe I never had it.
Although, I'd like to think that I was sexy.
Or at least others found me sexy...
...I hope!
Maybe I was just delusional.
If I never was sexy...
...then,
...I had nothing to lose?
Nevertheless...
...either way...
...I feel like I'm losing something...
...whether I had it or not!
'Cause...
...I feel like I'm losing sexuality!
In fact...
...I know,
...that I'm losing my sexuality.*

*Will I ever find it again?
I doubt it!*

"The Don"
04.06.2023

Superstitious

(Superstizioso)

Are you superstitious?
Do you *try to influence an outcome?*
Do you *carry out rituals to affect that outcome?*
Do you *try communicating to the "supernatural" to influence that outcome?*
Do *you turn to "Dark Magic" or the "Occult" to determine a favourable outcome...?*
...do you pray to God?
...do you worship the Devil to invervene & help you get...
...the outcome that you want?
...the outcome that you desire?
...the outcome that you would pay any price for?
...the outcome you would sacrifice everything for?
...even your soul?

If you do...
...then you are superstitious!

"Very superstitious,
Writing's on the wall,
Very superstitious,
Ladders bout' to fall,
Thirteen month old baby,
Broke the lookin' glass
Seven years of bad luck,
The good things in your past

When you believe in things
That you don't understand,
Then you suffer,
Superstition ain't the way

Superstition ain't the way,
No, no, no."

-"Superstitious"-Stevie Wonder

"The Don"
05.06.2023

Desperation for Salvation

(Disperazione per la Salvezza)

Why do we so desperately seek to be saved?
Who do we need to be saved from?
What do we need to be saved from?
Is it from *"Original Sin"*?
A sin apparently, I committed before I was even born!

Yet, we seek it *here...*
...we seek it *there,*
...we seek it *everywhere!*
We've been looking for it for a very long time.
But...
...we are STILL looking for it.
...searching for it.

We build monuments to this quest.
Great edifices that try to reach the heavens.
Built to last forever.
Adorned with such opulence that made one stand in awe.
Testaments to our desperate search for salvation.
This search, this quest, is it our *"Holy Grail"* that we seek?
Yet it is a forlorn sacrifice that we make.
While these edifies grow larger & more opulent...
...*we become weaker & poorer.*
Isn't it about time that we realise that this search is futile?
That there is never going to be an end.
Because...
...we do not need to be *saved!*
...we do not need *salvation!*
There is no salvation.
We have been lied to.
And we have accepted this lie as the *"Truth".*

Our *"Desperation for Salvation"* has all been in vain.
It has all been a waste of time & energy.
Only creating *"Human Suffering"* as a consequence.
Our *"Desperation for Salvation"* is now over!
No more...
..."*Desperation for Salvation*"
"*Desperation for Salvation*"
"*Desperation for Salvation*"
"*Desperation for Salvation*"

"The Don"
06.06.2023

Saved or Laid?

(Salvato o Ficcarerate)

Fucking is *FREEDOM!*
Fucking is *orgasmic!*
Fucking is *pleasurable!*
Fucking is *fun.*
Fucking *makes me happy.*

Fucking is *addictive!*
Fucking is a *drug!*
Fucking is a *chore!*
Fucking is a bore!
Fucking is a *disappointment!*
(although, it depends who with)
Fucking is *unnecessary!*
Fucking is *painful!*
Fucking *hurts!*
Fucking makes me sad.

Fucking causes *suffering.*
Fucking causes *craziness.*
Fucking causes *madness.*
Fucking causes *destruction.*
Fucking causes *stupidity.*
Fucking causes *idiocy.*
Fucking causes *INSANITY!*
Fucking makes me HIGH!

So, when fucking, are you...
...*saved or laid?*

"The Don"
06.06.2023

I Lie

(Non Dico la Verità)

I lie...
...and that's the "TRUTH"!

"The Don"
06.06.2023

I've Committed No Crime
(Non ho Commesso alcun Crimine)

I've completed my sentence.
But...
...I've committed no crime!

"We are the Champions"-Freddy Mercury
Performed by: Queen

"The Don"
07.06.2023

(Crescere!)

Grow up!

NO!

"The Don"
07.06.2023

I Haven't Cum Yet

(Non sono ancora Venuto)

Don't stop...
...I haven't come yet!

"The Don"
07.06.2023

Nothing's Changed...

(Non è Cambiato Niente...)

Nothing's changed.
But...
...everything's changed.

That's the paradox.

"The Don"
08.06.2023

BLOCK ME!

(Bloccami!)

Please BLOCK me!
Come on...
...FUCK you!
Just do it!

Let's get this over once & for all times...
...FUCKING BLOCK ME!

That way, you want get any of my messages on your posts...
...and I won't be able to stalk you.

"The Don"
07.06.2023

There is No Meaning

(Non C'è Significato)

We look for meaning in things when there is no meaning to be found!
Everything is *random*.
Everything is *unpredictable*.
Everything is *chaos*.
Everything is *meaningless*.
There is NO meaning.

Stop wasting your time & energy looking for something that doesn't exist.
Just accept that *there is NO meaning*.
Move on...
...*live your life*.
...*live in the moment*.
...*live for today*.
...*LO*❤*E the one you're with*.
Because...
...*there is NO meaning!*

"The Don"
09.06.2023

Self Liberation

(Autoliberazione)

Self *freedom*.
Self *discovery*.
Self *adventure*.
Self *journey*.
Self *determination*.
Self *liberation*.

Liberation from internal *conflicts*.
Liberation from internal *chaos*.
Liberation from internal *wars*.
Liberation from internal *divisions*.
Liberation from *mechanicity*.
Liberation from *determinism*.
Liberation from the *"Self"*!
That's...
...*Self liberation*.

"The Don"
09.06.2023

Who is Marisa deMatteo?

(Chi è Marisa de Matteo?)

I actually remember being in the same kindergarten class as her...
...a long time ago.
She was a *"Wog"*, just like me.
Then she disappeared.
I never saw her again for a very long time.
It was as if she disappeared from the face of the Earth.

Then she reappeared about 20 years later wondering the streets of Five Dock.
Bare foot, unkept, obviously homeless.
Like a wild, savage woman from the ghettoes.
Scavenging for food & bumming for cigarette butts.
She walked the streets of Five Dock, always alone...
...always looking the same, a wild unkept woman.
I never made eye contact.
Scared that she might stop & recognise me...
...maybe want to talk to me.
But she never stopped.

She used to sit at the bus-stop on Great North Road, in front of the bakery.
Then she would walk off & continue on her journey.
Sometimes I would see her wandering the streets of Haberfield, the adjoining suburb *(the Federation Suburb)*.
I've seen her travel as far as Leichhardt *(once known as "Little Italy")*, wandering the footpath of Parramatta Road, around from Norton Street.

She must have slept somewhere...
...eaten somewhere.
But I have no idea where.
Someone one told me that as a teenager, she fell in with the wrong people...
...a group of bikies.
...who mistreated her.
...abused her.
...used her.
And then abandoned her.
Apparently, her parents also abandoned her...
...and so, she roamed the streets.

You've probably seen her around, if you've ever been to Five Dock.
She is still roaming today...
...almost, 60 years later.
...and she still looks exactly the same...
...wild,
...unkept,
...bare footed,
...crazy eyed,
...feral
...homeless woman.

So, after all this time...
...the question still remains...
...who is Marisa deMateo?

But I haven't forgotten her.
I know who Marisa deMateo is!

"The Don"
11.06.2023

ONE DAY, HE'S GONNA EXPLODE

(Un Giorno, Sta per Esplodere)

One day, he's gonna explode.
I can see it.
Everyone can see.
It's *obvious*.
It's *so clear*.
One day, he's gonna explode.

He can't keep it bottled up inside for too much longer.
It's all gonna come out.
All that shit is gonna come gushing out.
One day, he's gonna explode.

He's a pressure cooker.
Trying to keep a lid on it.
Trying not to let anything escape.
That must take a lot of effort.
That must require a lot of energy.
But...
...one day, he's gonna explode.

He's got no sense of humour.
He can't laugh at himself.
He takes himself too seriously.
Fuck...
...he takes everything way too seriously
He's very *"heavy"*.
He's got a *"heavy"* load on his shoulders.
But...
...one day, he's gonna explode!

"The Don"
12.06.2023

How's Life Treating You?

(Come ti sta Trattando la Vita?)

How are you doing?
Are you ok?
Are you happy?
Are you doing the things you want to do?
Are you being creative?
So...
...how's life treating you?

What have you been up to?
Where have you been going?
Who have you been seeing?
Have you been doing anything interesting lately?
So...
...how's life treating you?

"The Don"
12.06.2023

When They're Awake, They're Asleep

(Quando sono Svegli, Dormono)

They are *walking*.
They are *moving about*.
They are *doing things*.
They are *talking*.
They even go to work.
But...
...they are not awake.
They are asleep.

I have to *wake them up.*
I have to *shake them up.*
I have to *shock them.*
I have to *shout at them...*
..."Hey, you!"
..."Yeah, you!"
..."Wake up!"
..."Yeah, I'm talking to you!"
..."Wake up!"
Because...
...when they're awake,
...they're asleep!

'Cause when you're awake, you're asleep.
Oh, YEAH!
Asleep!
Asleep!
Asleep!
Yeah!

When you're awake, you're asleep.
Oh, YEAH!
Asleep!
Asleep!
Asleep!
Yeah!

"The Don"
12.06.2023

Bad to the Bone

(Cattivo Fino il Ossi)

I'm *loud*.
I'm *rude*.
I'm *crude*.
I'm *lude*.
I'm *dirty*.
I'm *smutty*.
I'm *irreverent*.
I'm *sacrilegious*.
I'm *blasphemous*.
I'm *arrogant*.
I'm *disrespectful*.
I'm *agro*.
I'm *boisterous*.
I'm *uncouth*.
I'm *melodramatic*.
I'm a *raconteur*.
I'm a *trouble maker*.
I'm an *anarchist*.
I'm *political*.
I'm...
...bad to the bone.

I talk too *much*.
I talk too *loudly*.
I laugh too *loud*.
I stir *the pot*.
I cause *trouble*.

I say things that shouldn't be said.
I tell people things they don't want to hear.

I *smoke*.
I *drink*.
I *swear*...
...*a lot*.
I *swear*...
...*on purpose*.
I *take drugs*.

I *fart, in public, load & smelly & I blame others (if anyone's around)*.
Why?
Because...
...I'm bad to the bone.

"Bad to the bone, Bad to the bone
I'm B-B-B-B-Bad, B-B-B-B-Bad
B-B-B-B-Bad, I'm bad to the bone."

-*"Bad to the Bone"*
Songwriter: George Thorogood

"The Don"
12.06.2023

I Swear on the "Unholy" Bible
(Lo Giuro sulla Bibbia "Empio")

I swear on the "Unholy" bible.
I raise my left hand & put my right hand on it.
And say...
...I swear on this "Unholy" bible.

"The Don!
12.06.2023

I Have NOT Sold Myself to "A" God

(NON Mi Sono Venduto a "Uno" Dio)

"I have not sold myself to God!"

-Patti Smth-"Babelogue"-"Easter"

I have not sold myself to "A" God!

"The Don"
12.06.2023

Simple Minds
(Menti Semplici)

Simple *thoughts*.
Simple *ideas*.
Simple *curiousity*.
Simple *interests*.
Simple *intellect*.
Simple Minds.

Nothing too *deep*.
Nothing too *profound*.
Nothing too *complex*.
Nothing too *ethereal*.
Nothing too *spiritual*
Nothing too *esoteric*
For...
...*simple minds*.

No other *alternatives*.
No other *thoughts*.
No other *ideas*.
No other *interests*.
No other *paths*.
For...
...*simple minds*.

This is a *"Simple"* poem.
For...
...*simple minds*.

"The Don"
12.06.2023

𝕿ruth #2

(Verità #2)

Truth...
...what truth?
There is NO truth!

"The Don"
13.06.2023

The Battle of the Pussy & the Cock
(La Battaglia della Figa e del Cazzo)

You might think that the eternal battle is between *"Good" & "Evil"*.
But actually, it's always been between the *Pussy & the Cock!*
This battle has been going on since time immemorial.
A battle between these two great powers.
On one side we have the *Pussy*...
...and on the other side we have the *Cock*.
And in between lies the great divide.
This enormous chasm.
The Grand Canyon, you might say.

For the last 2000 years, the *Cock* has dominated.
But this has not always been the case.
There have been many civilisations throughout history in which the *Pussy*
was the dominant power.

Apparently, there are 5 Matriarchal societies...
..."India's Khasi Tribe. The state of Meghalaya in northeastern India is
home to the Khasi tribe, which is known for its matriarchal society. ...
...China's "Mosuo" People. ...
...Indonesia's "Minangkabau" People.
...Ghana's "Akan" People.
...Costa Rica's "Bribri" People.
(I had to "Google" this. I'm not that smart!)
All in the *"3rd World"*.
Definitely NOT in the 1st World!
Where the *Cock* still reigns supreme!
(Look at Trump & Putin & what they COCKS they are!)

Maybe, it is time for the *Pussy* to rise again...
...*to take control.*
...*to win the battle of the Pussy & the Cock.*

"The Don"
13.06.2023

What the FUCK are We Fighting For?
(Per Cazzo Cosa Stiamo Combattendo?)

What the FUCK are we fighting for?
Who the FUCK are we fighting for?
Well...
...it definitely ain't for you & me!

"What the hell are we fighting for?
We're waiting for the hammer to Fall!"

-"Hammer to fall!"-Brian May
-Performed by: Queen

"The Don"
14.06.2023

CONFRONT YOUR FEARS

(Affronta le Tue Paure)

Confront your fears.
That's what you've gotta do.
You can't *run away from them.*
You can't *hide from them.*
You can't *deny them.*
You can't *forget them.*
You just have to confront them.
Sooner or later...
...you have to confront your fears.

Don't fear them.
They'll ALWAYS be there...
...inside you.
Eating you from the inside.
Tearing you apart.
Driving you insane.
So...
...do it NOW!
Confront your fears!

Be *brave.*
Have *courage.*
Face them.
Look at them straight in the in the eyes...
...and confront them.
...whatever they are!

Don't let them *control you.*
Don't let them *define you.*
Don't let them *take over you.*
Don't let them *become you.*
Confront your fears...
...and defeat them.
...and then you will be free.
...FOREVER!

"The Don"
15.06.2023

POWER

(Potere)

The insaitable quest for power is insane.
We strive to control.
We want to command.
We seek to determine.
We desire to rule.
We create slaves.
We want power...
...we want power of others!

But this only produces violence.
We cannot control others.
We can only force others to do what we want...
...through the use of violence.

People do not want to be controlled.
People do not want to be ruled.
People do not want to be enslaved.
People do not want to be slaves.
People do not want power to be exercised over them.

You can NEVER have power over others!

You can ONLY have power over yourself.
You cannot have power of overs.
People want to be free to determine their own paths.
People want freedom.

The only power you can exercise is over yourself!

Power to yourself!
Power to yourself!
Power to yourself!
Power to yourself, right on!

"The Don"
17.06.2023

Mind's Eye

(L'occhio della Mente)

Mind's Eye.
Sometimes called the "Third Eye".
Scientifically called the "Pineal" gland.
Apparently, it is located somewhere slap bang in the middle of your brain.
It was known by the "Ancients".
There are icons of it all over the place...
...even on the "American Dollar Note".
...the famous "Greenback".
...the currency of the modern world.

Only a few special individuals can access its great power.
These are the true "Elders".
They are the ones that carry the "Ancient Knowledge".
They have the key...
...to unlock your "Mind's Eye".

Are you one?

I certainly am NOT!
But...
...I'm trying to understand the mysteries...
...of my "Mind's Eye".

"Eye!"
"Eye!"
In my "Mind's Eye".
In my "Mind's Eye".
In my "Mind's Eye".
In my "Mind's Eye".

"The Don"
17.06.2023

Wealth

(Ricchezza)

Wealth in monetary terms is just numbers.
It doesn't exist.
It's just a human construct.
It has no value other than the values we impose on it.
It doesn't have any intrinsic value of its own.
Not like spiritual wealth, which doesn't rely on external appreciation.
The value comes from *"within"*.
From deep inside one's self…
…*from deep within one's HE♥RT.*
…*from their very BEING.*
…*from their very ESSENCE.*

Which wealth do you seek?

I know which one I choose!

"Now give me money (that's what I want).
That's what I want.
That's what I waaaaant, that's what.

Money don't get you everything, it's true.
What it don't get, I can't use.
Now give me money (that's what I want).
That's what I waaaaaant.

I want money (that's want I want).
Now give me money (that's what I want).
That's what I waaaaaant."

-"Money (That's What I Want)-Barry Gordy Jr/Janie Bradford
-Performed by-The Beatles

"The Don"
17.06.2023

I'm Gonna Let Myself Indulge in Some Fantasises
(Mi Lascerò Indulgere in Alcune Fantasie)

I'm gonna let myself indulge in some fantasises.
Howzat!

"The Don"
17.06.2023

(é)

Ignorance is bliss.
Knowledge is power.
Intelligence is dangerous.
Imagination is freedom.
Thinking is forbidden.
Questioning is a crime.
Stupidity is unforgivable.
Reality is fake.
Subjectivity is reality.
Violence is control.
LO♥E is illusory.
Creativity is life.
Truth is subjective.
Life is Hell.
Death is final.

It is what it is!

"The Don"
19.06.2023

The Garden of Death

(Il Giardino della Morte)

I have a plot of land...
...it's not very big.
But…
...it's big enough.
But...
...no matter how hard I try to get something to grow there...
...nothing EVER does.
I've *tried EVERYTHING*.
I've *planted all varieties of seeds.*
But...
...NOTHING.
I've *watered them every day (sometimes, even twice a day).*
Still...
...NOTHING.
I didn't water them for a week...
...NOTHING.
I dug manure into the soil...
NOTHING.
I placed them in the sun...
...NOTHING.
I put them in the shade...
...NOTHING.
I talked to them...
...NOTHING.
I yelled abuse at them...
...NOTHING.
I played all genres of music to them...
...NOTHING.
I LO♥ED them...
...NOTHING.
I HATED them...
...NOTHING.

So, there was only one conclusion I could come too...
...it is "The Garden of DEATH"!

"The Don"
19.06.2023

No Limits

(Senza Limiti)

Do whatever you *want*.
Do whatever makes you *happy*.
Do whatever gives you *fulfilment*.
Do whatever gives you *purpose*.
Do whatever gives your life *meaning*.
My only suggestion to you is...
...also...
...do something that contributes to society's well-being...
...as a whole.
...do something that improves society.
...do something that makes the world a BETTER place.

Do think you can do that?

If you can...
...do it without limits.
Because...
...there are no limits!

"The Don"
19.06.2023

It's All Been Told Before
(È già Stato Detto Tutto)

It's all been told before.
But...
...it needs repeating!

"The Don"
19.06.2023

Utilitarianism

(Utilitarismo)

What is *"useful"* for a society?
What is *"required"* by a society?
What is *"helpful"* for a society?
What is *"needed"* by a society
To...
...function meaningfully?
...be sustainable?
...satisfy its basic needs?
...prosper?
...be happy?

Who gets to decide?
Only a *"select"* few...
The...
...elders?
...philosophers?
...lawyers?
...aristocracy?
...rich?
...workers?
...people?

This is the question.
Whomever you choose...
...choose wisely.
For...
...they are the ones that decide...
..."what type of society we live in"!

"The Don"
20.06.2023

Books written by "The Don"

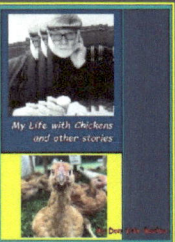

"My Life with Chickens & other stories: I Pity the Poor Immigrant"
*Published:
10th September, 2019
Autobiography Book 1:
0 – 12 years old*

"Poems for Misfits, Miscreants, Misanthropes, Mavericks, Losers & Malcontents!"
*Published:
10th June, 2020
Book of Poems 1*

"Poems for Troubled Minds & Trouble Hearts"
*Published:
10th August, 2020*

Book of Poems 2

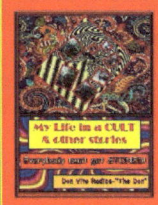

"My Life in a CULT & other stories: Everybody Must Get STONED!"
*Published:
10th September, 2020
Autobiography Book 2:
15 – 30 years old*

"Poems for Restless Minds & Restless Hearts"
*Published:
10th October, 2020*
Book of Poems 3

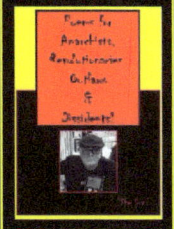

"Poems for Anarchists, Revolutionaries, Outlaws & Dissidents!"
*Published:
10th November, 2020*

Book of Poems 4

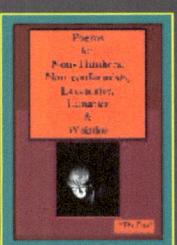

"Poems for Non-Thinkers & Eccentrics"
*Published:
10th December, 2020*
Book of Poems 5

"The Rantings of a Madman"
*Published:
10th January, 2021*

Book of Poems 6

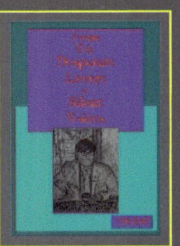

"Poems for Desperate Lovers & Silent Voices"
*Published:
10th February, 2021*
Book of Poems 7

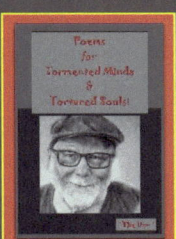

"Poems for Tormented Minds & Tortured Souls"
*Published:
10th March, 2021*
Book of Poems 8

All available ONLY online

Books written by "The Don"

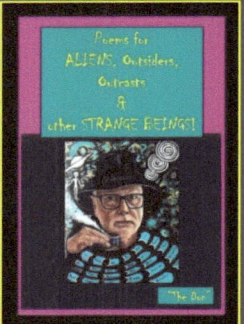

"Poems for ALIENS, Outsiders, Outcasts & other STRANGE BEINGS!"
Published: 10th April, 2021
Book of Poems 9

"Poems for Beings From Another Planet"
Published: 10th May, 2021
Book of Poems 10

"Poems for Mindless Beings & Lost Souls"
Published: 10th June, 2021
Book of Poems 11

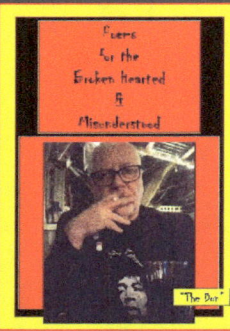

"Poems for the Broken Hearted & Misunderstood
Published: 10th July, 2021
Book of Poems 12

"Poems for Poems for the Bewildered, Dazed & Confused"
10th August, 2021
Book of Poems 13

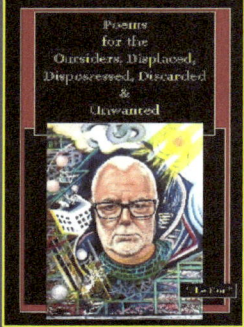

"Poems for the Outsiders, Displaced, Dispossessed, Discarded & Unwanted"
Published: 10th Sept, 2021
Book of Poems 14

All available ONLY online

"Poems for Secret Agents, Phantom Agents, Agents of Change, Agent Provocateurs & Agents of Chaos"
Published: 10th Oct, 2021
Book of Poems 15

"Poems for Disenchanted, Disillusioned & Delusional"
Published: 10th November, 2021
Book of Poems 16

Books written by "The Don"

"Poems for the Stoners, drugos, ACID takers & Psychedelic LO♥ERS (Everybody Must Get Stoned)"
Published: 10th December, 2021
Book of Poems 17

"Poems for Anarchists, Rebels & Revolutionaries
Published: 10th January, 2022
Book of Poems 18

"Poems for Rebels, Radicals & Revolutionaries (Viva la Révolution!)"
Published: 10th February, 2022
Book of Poems 19

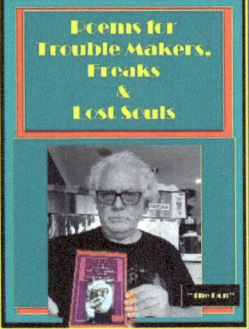

"Poems for Trouble Makers, Freaks & Lost Souls"
Published: 10th March 2022
Book of Poems 20

"Poems for Zombies & the Walking Dead"
Published: 10th April 2022
Book of Poems 21

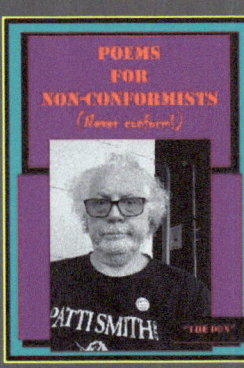

"Poems for Non-Conformists (Never conform!)"
Published: 10th May 2022
Book of Poems 22

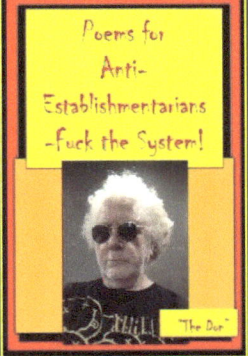

"Poems for Anti-Establishmentarians -Fuck the System!"
Published: 10th June 2022
Book of Poems 23

"Poems for the Voiceless"
Published: 10th July 2022
Book of Poems 24

All available ONLY online

Books written by "The Don"

"Poems for the Fearless"

Published: 10th August 2022

Book of Poems 25

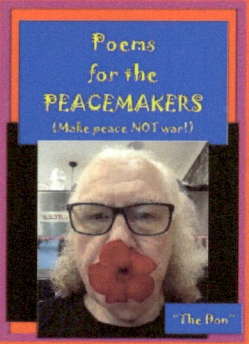

"Poems for the PEACEMAKER: Make peace NOT war!"

Published: 10th March 2023

Book of Poems 26

Poems for the Forever Young (May you stay forever young!)
Published: 10th June 2023
Book of Poems 27

Poems for the Children of the REVOLUTION!
Published: 5th December 2023

Book of Poems 28

Poems for the L'Innocente!
Published:
10th March 2024
Book of Poems 29

All available ONLY online

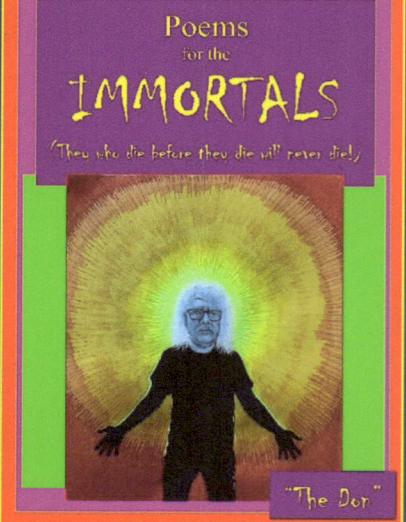

Poems for the IMMORTALS (They who die before they die will never die!)
Published: 10th September 2024
Book of Poems 30

www.ingramcontent.com/pod-product-compliance
Lightning Source LLC
Chambersburg PA
CBHW041502010526
44107CB00049B/1628